THE ART OF BREWING BEER

by Mark Henry

THE ART OF BREWING BEER

by Mark Henry

A Fireside Book
Published by Simon & Schuster

FIRESIDE
Rockefeller Center
1230 Avenue of the Americas
New York, New York 10020

FIRESIDE and colophon are registered trademarks
of Simon & Schuster Inc.

The Art of Brewing Beer is produced by becker&mayer!, Ltd.
From *The Art of Brewing Beer* packaged set, which includes beer
brewing ingredients, tools, and this book.

Designed by Julie Sullivan
Printed in Canada

10 9 8 7 6 5 4 3 2 1

Library of Congress Cataloging-in-Publication data is available.

ISBN 0-684-81882-5

Contents

Introduction

My introduction to home brewing began with a chance encounter with what was to become one of the signature beers of the Pacific Northwest. In 1982 I was an impressionable young college student at the University of Oregon. In typical college student fashion, a few classmates and I chose to celebrate the completion of another semester at one of the local pubs, where we were offered an unusual beer from a brewery we had never heard of. Several Redhooks later, my friends and I were talking about dropping out of school and starting a brewery.

With some small measure of regret, we never did actually forsake school for commercial beer brewing, but I did take the step of trying to learn about the brewing process. In 1982 brewing literature was rare and antiquated, and usually required a chemistry

degree to understand; unfortunately, I was a liberal arts student, so my early attempts at brewing were not altogether successful.

By 1985, however, small breweries had sprung up all along the West Coast. My hometown of Portland, Oregon, boasted no less than five breweries, as well as numerous brewpubs. Inspired, I dusted off my old fermenters and resumed my brewing career.

A sense of urgency set in when my first love, Redhook Ale, stopped being produced on a regular basis. If I was to enjoy a steady supply of the elixir of my youth, I was going to have to create it myself. Fortunately, by this time the art and science of small-scale brewing had been made easier by the publication of a book called *The Complete Joy of Homebrewing*. It took the prevailing knowledge of brewing and made it understandable to the average liberal arts college graduate.

For the last ten years I have been producing at home what is arguably the best beer I've ever drunk, and have gone so far as to open and operate the kind of brewing-supply store I wish had been available in 1982. I have never succeeded in replicating the original Redhook Ale, but then I'm fairly certain the Redhook Brewery will probably never succeed in making any beers like mine either.

The History of Beer

Many archaeologists believe beer to be responsible for the advent of civilization. My take on this theory is that during the hunting and gathering period of history, one of our ancestors discovered that the grain that had been painstakingly gathered and stored had gotten wet and smelly, but life being what it was 8,000 years ago, this grain was eaten anyway. For a while our ancestor found that life was not so nasty, brutish, and short. On the contrary, he had finally discovered something worth settling down for! Organized cultivation of grain began so as to assure a steady supply of grain for beer making. With farming came communities, industrialized society, and, a bit later, the neighborhood pub.

Of course, the "beer" being produced in the early days bore but a slight resemblance to Redhook Ale. It was no doubt tainted by a multitude of beer-spoiling microorganisms, forcing the ancients to spice it up some to make consumption tolerable. Beers were often spiced with heather or other herbs to add an agreeable flavor. Fortunately, considerable progress has been made in brewing beer in the intervening years. Today we understand that the central component in converting grains into a fermented beverage is a single-celled microorganism called yeast. By controlling the activity of yeast, and by preventing other microorganisms from invading our beer, we can create the kind of high-quality product that eluded those first brewers.

As a result of cultural, agricultural, and geographical differences, many styles of beer have been developed over the years. Despite this, beer can be divided into two basic categories: ale and lager. These two types can be further described as top-fermenting (ale) and bottom-fermenting (lager), terms that refer to the way different yeast strains react in fermentation. In general, top-fermenting ales typify the beers made in England, the wheat beer made in Germany, and the beers made by many small breweries in America. Bottom-fermenting lagers got their start in Germany and Bohemia, where they are the dominant beer type. Indeed, bottom-fermenting lagers are the most brewed beer type in the world.

Top-fermenters

Until the mid-1800s, ales were the most commonly brewed beers in the world. Artificial refrigeration was not yet available, and ale yeasts work well at ambient temperatures. The original ales were dark, murky, full bodied, and by today's standards very strong in flavor. Britain's colonial policies helped spread the popularity of and techniques for brewing the typical British ale. The fact that British soldiers had a right to a measured amount of ale per day helped ensure its availability throughout the country's colonies.

Today, British-style ales vary in color, strength, and bitterness. The bitterness and aroma in beer come from the amount and type of hops that are added to the brew. The beer brewer is constantly trying to strike a balance of just the right combination of hops. (For more information about hops, see page 16.) Pale ales are dark golden to copper in color and moderately to heavily bittered, and range in strength from 3% to 6% alcohol content. Brown ales, and their cousin the Scottish ale, are reddish to dark brown in color, lightly bittered, and medium in strength. Porters and stouts, on the other hand, are probably the most misunderstood of the ales, because some of these intimidating dark beers are mild in strength and body. For example, Guinness, the epitome of a stout, weighs in at a mere 4.2% alcohol content despite a foreboding opacity. Stouts and porters are closely related, with the primary difference being the bittering (stouts have more) and the use of coffeelike roasted barley (again, stouts use more). Stouts are opaque, whereas porters range from a translucent dark brown to opaque. But both are very rich in texture and flavor.

Another major ale style, and one that is increasingly popular in the United States, is wheat beer. These beers are Bavarian in origin and commonly go by the name of Hefeweizen—which is simply German for "wheat beer with yeast." They are generally light in color and body, composed of 50% to 70% wheat, and are very lightly bittered. Most commercial examples made in the United States are low to medium in alcohol strength, and are meant as a refreshing alternative to heavier ales.

BOTTOM-FERMENTERS

Before 1841 there was no top-fermenting/bottom-fermenting dichotomy, because different yeasts had not yet been identified. That year, however, an enterprising German brewer discovered that the smooth, clean beers brewed by

Bavarian monasteries were the result of a yeast strain that fermented cleanly and completely and then settled out well. This yeast worked best when fermented at the cooler temperatures found in most high-altitude monasteries. The German took this strain back to his own brewery and started brewing what came to be known as lager beers.

The use of this bottom-fermenting lager yeast quickly spread throughout continental Europe. At about the same time, clear glass mugs, instead of traditional metal or ceramic mugs, came into widespread use. Now that drinkers could see their beer before they quaffed, a preference for a beer with a high degree of clarity developed. The introduction of refrigeration into commercial brewing allowed warmer climates to ferment lagers, and this meant that the Bavarian monks lost their hold on this tasty monopoly. The stage was now set for lagers to become the choice of beer drinkers worldwide.

Many types of lager have been developed over the years—pilsners, bocks, Viennas, helles, and dunkles—each with its own characteristics. The most popular style of lager today is the pilsner; indeed, most of the beer produced commercially in the United States is a lightly bittered version of the traditional pilsner. European pilsners are bittered more, and the original pilsner, Pilsner Urquell, is very bitter. Another distinctive lager is bock beer.

Contrary to popular opinion, bocks are not produced by the dregs of the beer tank, although they may give that impression since they are traditionally dark, rich, and fairly high in alcohol. Vienna-style beers, on the other hand, and their cousins the Oktoberfest beers, are amber lagers rich in flavor. Interestingly, the best-known commercial example of this type of beer is Mexican-brewed Negra Modelo. In Bavaria, where lager brewing got its start, Münchner-style lagers are most common and are referred to as either helles (light) or dunkle (dark) beers. These beers have a malty character and are very lightly bittered.

RECENT HISTORY

Two events had considerable impact on beer style in the United States. The first was the immigration of central Europeans into the United States in the mid-1800s. With this influx came the German and Bohemian influence on brewing and consumption. Although commercial brewing was still very localized in the seventeenth century, strong brewing communities had developed in Wisconsin, New York, and California. The introduction of lager brewing by these new citizens resulted in an interesting mixture of techniques. Porter, for example, ordinarily a top-fermenting draft, was brewed with bottom-fermenting yeasts at Yuengling's brewery in Pennsylvania. New styles of beer such as the California common were also created during this time. Known colloquially as "steam" beers, the California common style is a testimony to American ingenuity and Americans' undying thirst for beer. Developed before the widespread use of refrigeration, this beer was created when brewers in the warm California climate produced lagers at ale temperatures, then cold-stored them to develop a crisp, clean flavor. Fritz Maytag's Anchor Steam Beer is the best-known example of this beer, amber in color, medium-bodied, generously hopped, and with a robust flavor resulting from the higher fermentation temperature.

The second event that strongly influenced American beer styles was Prohibition, which indelibly altered the brewing industry. By the end of this social experiment in 1933, only the largest, strongest companies had survived—by making root beer, soda pop, and non-alchoholic beers. This concentration of the industry into a few hands resulted in relatively nondescript beers being produced, with national marketability a major element of the brewers' recipes. Indeed, for the next forty-five years, almost all the beer produced in the United States was a variation on a light, effervescent, low-bittered pilsner.

In 1978, however, the New Albion brewery in northern California fired the shot heard all the way to Milwaukee when it started producing the first example of what was to become known as "craft beer." Today, there are over three hundred small American breweries serving local markets with a dizzying variety of beers. As individual states adjust their laws to allow microbrewery operations, and as consumers develop a taste for different types of beers, the number of small breweries continues to grow.

What's in a Beer?

There are more than sixty styles and substyles of beer, each with its own distinct flavor profile. For all the variation, however, beer contains just four primary ingredients: water, malted grain, hops, and yeast. According to the German Reinheitsgebot (Purity Law) of 1516, beer produced in Germany can contain only these four ingredients; many breweries in other countries also adhere to these precepts. Understanding what each of these ingredients are and how they affect the flavor of the drink is essential to understanding the art of brewing beer. But the process is complex. The brewer has more than forty different malts, thirty-five different hops, and thirty different yeast strains to work with. It may take a chemist and a statistician to calculate all the potential variations, but it is the artist who brings them all together. A well-made beer is indeed greater than the sum of its parts.

Water

Brewers can be divided into two groups: artists and chemists. While all brewers exhibit some characteristics of both groups, how a brewer approaches the use of water in beer really defines in which camp a brewer belongs. That water is of the utmost importance in beer cannot be denied—after all, beer is 92% water. An artistic brewer understands this, and then forgets about it. As long as the possibility of chlorine contamination is dealt with, the local water supply is regarded as perfectly fine. This, after all, is how pre–Industrial Revolution brewers addressed the use of water. The chemist, on the other hand, wants to know exactly what is in the water and how it will affect the finished product. She or he may also want to know how to duplicate the composition of the water from certain brewing regions of the world. The harder water in some areas of England, for instance, helps accentuate the hops characteristics of a pale ale, while the very soft water in the Czech town of Pilsen complements the soft edges of a Bohemian pilsner.

Pure water is simply H_2O, but in real life water includes a host of other minerals. And each of these minerals can have a dramatic effect on the three other central components of beer. Where brewing is concerned, one of the most important minerals found in water is calcium. To some degree, calcium levels will dictate how a malt is used and whether a beer is sharp in flavor or smoother and well rounded. In most lager-type beers, low levels of calcium are desired. The inverse is true of British ales. Other important minerals commonly found in water are sodium, magnesium, and chloride (not to be confused with chlorine). Magnesium is a valuable yeast nutrient, while sodium and chloride both contribute a "sweet spot" to beer. If your water is suitable for consumption, it will undoubtedly be suitable for brewing beer. Eliminating chlorine with a pre-use boiling or filtering procedure is the only advance preparation necessary.

Grain

So what is the relationship between the water that constitutes so much of beer and the grain that determines much of a beer's character and flavor? To be suitable for brewing beer, the grain has to be allowed to germinate and then be cured, a process called "malting." Grains that have been taken through the malting process are then generally referred to simply as "malt." (The most common malt used in beer is barley malt, although wheat and rye are also used.) When the brewmaster steeps malts in water at 148–155°F, enzyme action occurs that converts most of the starch in the barley into sugars. In brewing parlance, this is known as "mashing" the grains. These sugars are then rinsed out of the malt and into the brewpot, where the sweet liquid, now called wort (pronounced "wert"), is boiled for an hour or so.

There are well over forty different varieties of malted barley, and each will impart a unique flavor to beer. Stouts and porters get their dark color and roasted bite from a brewmaster's liberal use of malts that were roasted much like espresso coffee beans. Malts that have been caramelized are a central component of the richer, sweeter British ales. And the delicate flavor of many lager beers is created by using malts that undergo an arrested germination process. In order to make small-scale brewing easier, in recent years malting companies have started producing high-quality, ready-to-use "malt extracts" for brewing. The wort created by this process is vacuum-boiled down to a syrup, which the home brewer reconstitutes with brewing water. Depending upon how the malt extract was created, this reconstituted wort may then be boiled, although some extracts do not require this.

Hops

Before the year 1400 there was no consensus on whether hops ought to be used in beer at all. Not until just a few hundred years ago was opposition to the use of this herb overcome. Originally hops were added for their antibacterial properties, since a beer with hops was less likely to spoil. Eventually consumers came to appreciate the balancing effect hops bitterness had on the sugar sweetness of unhopped beer, and today a fermented beverage without hops would not be considered beer. So great has the affection for the hoppy flavor grown, in fact, that in today's brewing world, radical factions of brewers called "hopheads" believe a beer cannot be too hoppy or bitter. Fortunately, they are mostly isolated to the hops-growing regions of the Pacific Northwest.

Over thirty-five different varieties of hops exist, and each contributes differently to the bitterness of beer. Large breweries prefer hops with high bitterness potential, so they can use less of them per amount produced. Small-scale brewers tend to be more creative, selecting hops based on the flavor and aromatic properties of a particular variety. Although many small brewers experiment with hops, some hops are considered traditional for certain styles of beer. The spicy quality of Czech Saaz hops is prized in most European pilsners. Cascade hops, a popular North American type with a citrusy flavor and aroma, are used in Sierra Nevada Pale Ale, among other beers.

Hops must be boiled in the wort to extract bitterness and flavor. The time and length of the boil will affect both the level of bitterness and the hoppy flavor the beer will have. The aromatic qualities of hops are volatile and fleeting, so either a very short boil or a postboil steep is all that is required to give beer a fine hoppy aroma. Experimentation with different varieties and boiling times is easy and yields widely varying results, and it is through hops usage that the artistic nature of a brewer is usually revealed.

Yeast

Without yeast, there would be no beer. These living microorganisms meld all the other components of beer into one, imparting a flavor or two of their own. As yeast consumes sugar it excretes ethanol alcohol, carbon dioxide, which carbonates the beer; fusel alcohols, which are often blamed for hangovers; and a host of chemical compounds that provide beer with much of its complexity. Beer yeast is added—or pitched, in brewing parlance—as soon as the boiled wort is cooled to less than 80°F. Within 12 hours, fermentation starts and beer is born.

When selecting a yeast, the brewer will first consider whether a top-fermenting ale strain or a bottom-fermenting lager strain is needed. The yeast is then tested in small batches to see if the finished beer has the flavor profiles desired. Small-scale brewers generally have ready access to thirty or forty different beer yeast strains.

Fermentation

Many variables influence both the progress of the fermentation and the quality of the finished product, but the most important of these is temperature. High-temperature fermentation, 65–75°F, causes yeast to ferment faster and create more of the chemical compounds known collectively as esters. Esters have subtle, and sometimes not so subtle, fruity flavors. As an extreme example of the impact of esters, a few years ago a brewery made a name for itself with a blueberry lager beer that had no blueberries in it—the yeast they used created an excess of blueberry-flavored esters. A lower temperature for fermentation, 45–55°F, tends to make the process take longer and produce fewer esters. This results in a beer that may have fewer flavor notes but is cleaner and crisper.

BREWING

The production of beer has been marked by continuous evolution. Whereas our ancestors combined a few ingredients, prayed to the patron saint of brewers, Gambrinus, and hoped for the best, large modern breweries engage in nothing less than biological manipulation to achieve a desired product. Small-scale brewing occupies a middle ground. Still, whether the scale of operation is one gallon or two hundred, the basic processes are similar. With this kit, you will be producing a medium-bodied, lightly hopped British-type amber ale of the sort popular with many of North America's small breweries. It will contain approximately 4% alcohol.

Contents of Your Kit

1 POUND ALEXANDER'S
HOPPED MALT SYRUP

1 THREE-GRAM PACKAGE
RED STAR ALE YEAST

1 AIRLOCK WITH BORED
RUBBER STOPPER

1 LENGTH SIPHONING TUBING

BREWING INSTRUCTIONS

BEFORE YOU BREW

Before proceeding, you will also need an aluminum or stainless steel pot capable of holding at least 1½ gallons of wort, a kitchen funnel, 1 gallon jug of good bottled water, and a 1-gallon glass jug (many table wines are available in this size glass container). This jug will be used with the airlock and stopper to pitch the yeast and ferment the beer. Bring your stopper along when looking for a jug; you'll need a container with a narrow mouth. For bottling, you will need ¼ cup of granulated sugar or ⅛ cup of honey. You will also need at least six bottles. Although there are many types you can use, the most convenient are 12-ounce plastic soda pop bottles. You can also use 1-liter soda bottles (at least two) or Grolsche-type resealable beer bottles (about six). If you've collected all the items you need, let's brew some beer.

Other Supplies That Might Be Useful

Home brewers traditionally brew in 5-gallon increments. The fermentation vessel most often used is a 5-gallon glass water bottle or carboy. If a carboy is being used, a rigid piece of tubing called a racking cane is used to draw out the beer. When brewing and bottling in these volumes, regular refillable beer bottles are usually used. Five gallons of beer will fill forty-eight 12-ounce bottles. Putting beer into bottles is made easier by the use of a bottle filler, which is spring-loaded and allows a mess-free fill. A capper for adhering bottle caps to bottles will be required, the most common type being a wing or double-lever capper. All professional brewers and most avid home brewers track fermentation-induced density changes using a hydrometer, which enhances the repeatability of results.

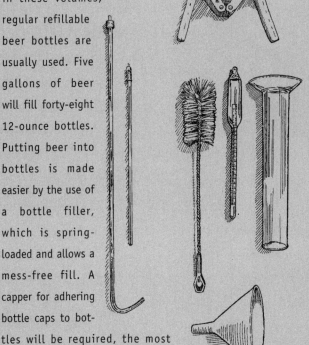

Boiling the Wort

First, pour the gallon of water into your pot, top up with 2 additional cups of tap water, and heat to just below boiling. Removing the pot from the heat, add your hopped malt syrup. (A little hint: If you preheat the can in some warm water, the syrup will flow out easier.)

Once the syrup is completely dissolved into the brewing water, place the pot back on the heating element. With the temperature on medium, boil the wort for 30 minutes, watching the pot carefully. Apply only as much heat as is necessary to keep a slow boil, since too high a temperature will cause caramelization of the sugars in the malt and will create a beer that is very dark and overly sweet.

Once the wort comes to a boil, you may get some pretty intense foaming for a few minutes, the result of the coagulation of proteins

in the malt. This is desired. Of course, wort all over your stove is not. If the foaming is so intense that a boil-over is imminent, lift the pot off the element, turn the heat to low, and put the pot back on the element. The foaming will be over shortly, and you will then be able to resume your boil.

Boiling the wort is necessary because good protein coagulation will result in a cleaner-tasting beer with good clarity. Boiling also sterilizes the wort, and if hops are being added to a beer, the boiling process extracts the flavorful oil from the hops.

After you are done boiling the wort, put a lid on the pot and allow the wort to cool to room temperature. It is important to limit the cooling wort's exposure to air.

Sanitizing Your Equipment

Because nobody brews in a laboratory environment, potential contact with airborne microorganisms should be minimized. This is a good time to begin sanitizing everything that will come into contact with the wort. Begin with the gallon glass jug. Pour 1 tablespoon of common household bleach, preferably unscented, into the jug and fill with cold water. Allow this to sit for at least half an hour to kill any microorganisms in the jug. Then empty the jug into your stoppered sink and soak the airlock, rubber stopper, and funnel in the bleach solution for half an hour. After soaking these items, rinse everything, including the jug, thoroughly with hot tap water.

Pitching the Yeast

The wort is probably cool enough now to put into the glass jug. Using the sanitized funnel, carefully pour the wort into the jug, filling it to within 3 inches from the top. Discard any wort that may still be in the pot. Check the temperature of the

wort by placing your hand on the side of the jug. If it is warm to the touch, it is still too hot to pitch your yeast. In this case, affix the airlock to the rubber stopper and plug it into the jug. Now pour 1½ teaspoons of water into the top of the airlock. This creates a barrier that allows gas to exit the jug but does not allow air in. (Actually, I like to put vodka in the airlock because it is sterile.)

Once the jug is cool to the touch, tear open a corner of the yeast package and carefully remove the airlock from the jug. Pour the granulated yeast into the jug and replace the airlock. From now until you bottle it, it is important that your fermenting beer be kept in a dark, cool place where it will not be disturbed. Optimal fermentation temperature is between 62°F and 72°F, although temperatures up to 78°F can be tolerated.

Fermentation Begins

At this point patience is all that is necessary. It is after the yeast is pitched, however, and before signs of active fermentation appear, that brewers worry the most. Mother hens have nothing on new brewers. Don't despair. Fermentation can take as few as two days or as many as ten, but within 24 hours you will see a froth start to form on the surface of the wort. This is an indicator of yeast activity and a sign that all is well. Bubbling will also appear in your airlock as the carbon dioxide that builds up in the jug escapes. At the height of fermentation your airlock could bubble as often as once a second. You will know fermentation is done when activity in the airlock drops to a bubble every 2 minutes or less. The wort is now called "green beer," and it shouldn't be too cloudy at this point. If it still looks cloudy, and fermentation took only a few days, there is no harm in letting it sit for a few more days to clarify. Even if your green beer remains cloudy, you should bottle it within ten days of the start of fermentation.

Making Your Beer Truly Your Own

One of the most enjoyable aspects of your new hobby is deciding on a brewery name, with corresponding labels for your
bottles. "Webfoot Brewing Company" is my brewery name, with
each of my creations named after University of Oregon football
and track stars of yore. "Bad Dog Brewery" and "Imperial Wort
Processing Company" are some friends' examples. With the easy
availability of desktop publishing, designing your own label is
easy. The same gum-backed paper that breweries use is available and is laser-printable. It is always considered bad form to
serve your beer in bottles with someone else's labels still on
them, so soak off those labels, design your own, and present
your beer with pride!

Preparing the Bottles

The key to quick, trouble-free bottling is to be prepared. Before proceeding with bottling, be sure that all your bottles and bottling equipment are clean and sterilized. This is vital because any bacterial contaminant on your equipment will foul your beer. The easiest sanitizing solution is household bleach and water mixed in a ratio of about 1 part bleach to 200 parts water (1 to 2 ounces bleach to 5 gallons of water). After you wash out your bottles, soak them along with the caps and hosing in a stronger solution of ¼ cup of bleach to 4 or 5 gallons of cold water—a kitchen sink works well for this job. After a half-hour soak you will need to rinse everything thoroughly with warm tap water. This is important, since the taste of chlorine bleach can be detected in beer at levels as low as 5 parts per million. Also, be sure you have more bottles prepared than you will actually need. Racing around trying to find just one more bottle is not conducive to a positive bottling experience.

Adding the Sugar

After you have rinsed everything, you will need to add a small amount of sugar or honey to each bottle. This is done to stimulate a secondary fermentation in the bottle, creating carbon dioxide. If the bottles are well-sealed, the CO_2 will have nowhere to go and will be reabsorbed into the beer, thereby carbonating it. The level of carbonation is dictated by the amount of sugar or honey you add. Adding $1/2$ teaspoon or $1/4$ teaspoon honey per 12-ounce bottle is the norm. If you add a bit more, you will increase the level of carbonation. Be careful, though: Too much sugar or honey—for example, 1 teaspoon of sugar per 12-ounce bottle—and the bottle could explode. If you are using 16-ounce bottles, up to 1 teaspoon of sugar or $1/2$ teaspoon of honey is acceptable; with 1-liter bottles you can use up to 2 teaspoons of sugar or 1 teaspoon of honey. But be sure to keep track of which bottles you have added the sugar or honey. If you dose a bottle twice, the results will definitely be undesirable.

FILLING THE BOTTLES

At this point it is important to work as quickly as possible to prevent possible airborne contaminants from affecting your beer. Place your jug a couple of feet above the bottles (or the bottles a couple of feet below the jug). Remove the airlock and insert the siphoning hose until it is just short of the sediment on the bottom of the jug. It will now be necessary to start a siphon.

There are volumes written about starting siphons, but unless you have access to a sterile self-enclosed pump, I suggest the old-fashioned way. Gargle with a little vodka to remove any contaminants from your mouth (it is okay to swallow it), and suck on the end of the hose until you start to draw beer. Crimp the hose about 1 foot from the end and place the hose into your first bottle. Let it go and fill your bottle to about ¼ inch from the top. A little lower or higher is not a problem. Once your bottle is filled, recrimp the hose to shut off the flow, and set a cap loosely on top of the bottle to keep contaminants out. Move on to the next bottle, and start the process over. Remember to always keep your eyes on the bottle you are filling, because bottles often fill up faster than expected. After all of the bottles are full, go back to each one and screw the cap on tight. (As you move from one bottle to the next, you may get the idea that the larger bottles are easier to fill. The downside is that you'll have to drink more beer once those bottles are opened.)

As you are filling your bottles, you may draw up some of the sediment from the bottom of the jug. While it is best to avoid this, a little sediment in the bottom of your bottles will not have a great effect on the beer. In fact, naturally carbonated beer such as yours will always have a small amount of sediment in the bottom of each bottle anyway.

And Now the Wait...

After the bottling process comes the really, really hard part of brewing beer, when the beer goes through a three- to four-week period of carbonating and conditioning. During this time it is once again necessary to keep your beer in a dark, cool environment. And no peeking. Beer that has not been allowed to condition properly will often have a "green," harsh flavor. With time this will diminish, leaving behind a nice effervescent ale. When a few weeks have passed and you are ready to sample the fruits (or, more accurately, the grains) of your labor, simply refrigerate a bottle for an hour or so, decant it into a glass, and enjoy. *Prosit!*

TROUBLESHOOTING GUIDE

Brewing beer is not an exact science. The beers that we love and consume today took hundreds of years to develop. No doubt, along the way a lot of undesirable beer was produced. There are things that can and do go wrong for both commercial and amateur brewers. Quite frankly, dumping beer because something went awry is not practiced enough by some commercial brewers, leading to surprised consumers when a beer does not taste like it did the time before. As a consumer it can be invaluable to know what some of the more common beer faults are. As a home-brewer it is important to know how they are caused, and how to correct them.

THE MOST COMMON PROBLEMS ENCOUNTERED WITH BEER

CLOYING SWEETNESS

A typical difficulty encountered by inexperienced brewers, it is generally noticeable as a caramel-sweet flavor that detracts from the cleanness of the beer's taste. An overly long or too aggressive boil will cause excessive carmelization of the sugars in the wort. This will result in your beer taking on a dark amber color. If carmelization is a problem, reduce the vigorousness of the boil. As the beer conditions in the bottle this flavor profile will also decrease.

Cardboard Flavor

This problem is caused by oxidization after fermentation. Because stale beer will take on a cardboard/papery flavor, it is important to treat beer gently after fermentation is finished. Avoid splashing when filling bottles.

Storing your beer in a warm place will speed up oxidization. Your beer is best stored at 55–65°F.

Medicinal Flavors

Medicinal flavors are usually caused by chlorophenols, which in turn are created primarily by the presence of chlorine (from sterilizing or from chlorinated water). If chlorophenols are a problem, be sure you are rinsing your equipment well after sanitizing it. Pre-boiling tap water prior to brewing will reduce the chlorine taste, as will using filtered or bottled drinking water.

Metallic Flavors

A metallic flavor in your beer is most often caused by iron, zinc, or other metal ions in the water. First look to your water supply. If this is the culprit you will need either to filter your water or change your source of brewing water. If you are working with an enameled pot, you should also check it for scratches and chips, and if either exist, retire the pot. Some people also report picking up a metallic taste if an aluminum pot is used.

Sour or Tart Flavors

This problem is caused by bacteria, usually *acetobacter* or *lactobacilli* bacteria. They won't hurt you, but they can make beer taste awful. Visually a bacterial infection will leave a "bathtub ring" in the bottle at the beer line and make your beer very cloudy. Bacteria problems can be handled by ensuring sound sanitation techniques. Always sanitize everything that will come into contact with the beer after the boil.

Haze

Haze is only considered a problem if you prefer your beer crystal clear. A haze can be caused by the presence of starch and/or tannins. When you start to work more with raw ingredients this may become an issue. Typically, "fining agents" such as isinglass (dried powdered sturgeon swim bladder—really!) or gelatin are added to the beer a day or so before bottling to eliminate haze.

Soapy Taste

A soapy character in a beer is caused by the presence of excessive fatty acids. When beer is in contact with yeast longer than desired, the yeast will break down, or autolyze, and release fatty acids. Be sure your fermentation does not stay in the primary fermenter longer than ten days.

No Head

A lack of a head is usually associated with little or no carbonation. Assuming sufficient priming sugar was added at bottling time, this can be caused by a bad seal on the caps. It may be necessary to re-prime the bottle and replace the cap.

No Head Retention

If you get a good head of foam on your beer initially but it dissipates rapidly, look to your cleaning procedures. Do not use dishwashing detergents since they almost all leave a residue that will kill the head on beer.

Foaming

Beer that foams or, worse, gushes out of the bottle when you open it could be caused by one of four things:

1. Bottling prematurely—if beer has not finished fermenting you will have over-carbonated beer.

2. Bacteria (see "Sour or Tart Flavors," on page 37).

3. The addition of too much priming sugar at bottling time.

4. Your drinking buddy shook up the bottle and put it back in the fridge.

Special note: If your beer has an undefinable flavor that you can't place but that definitely does not appeal to you, be patient, especially if the brew is relatively young. You will see a very perceptible change from week to week in the flavor of your beer. With a little time it will come around. Time will cure many beer ills.

Let's Do It Again

By now, you have successfully produced a gallon of an amber ale. Congratulations! Take a moment to pat yourself on the back and enjoy a mug of your brew. If you're satisfied with your first effort, getting the ingredients to replicate the beer you just made is a snap. And the equipment in this kit can be reused repeatedly to make the beer you are now drinking, as well as a host of variations to suit any palate.

Most brewing supply retailers (see "Resources," page 52) will carry cans of hopped malt extract. The malt extract provided in this kit is Alexander's; it is an excellent choice, but not normally available in a pre-hopped form. Munton & Fison is, in my opinion, the best hopped malt extract obtainable. If you cannot find Munton & Fison, there are over 20 other malt extract producers, most of whom make a quality product. A good malt extract will list ingredients. Make sure the ingredients include only malt extract and water (and hops, if you are purchasing the pre-hopped extract). Most malt extract producers also date-stamp their cans; be sure to look for it. Also, the home-brewing connoisseur should take note that British malt extracts will produce fuller-bodied beers while North American malt extracts make cleaner, lighter beers.

In your first batch of beer, you used a hopped malt extract syrup, one of three kinds of malt extract. Your two other choices are unhopped malt extract syrup and unhopped malt extract powder. Each has its own advantages. The hopped syrup is obviously the easiest route to take. The unhopped syrup allows the more artistic brewmaster to experiment with one of the 35 varieties of hops discussed earlier in this book. The unhopped dry extract has a longer shelf life and also allows the brewer to select the hops. A disadvantage is that if you neglect to add hops to an unhopped extract, nothing will provide the necessary bitterness to balance the malt sweetness of the beer and you will end up with a rather unpalatable sickly sweet brew.

I am not aware of any hopped syrup extracts available in any size other than 3.3-pound cans. When you purchase the hopped malt extract syrup, it's a good idea to divide the liquid into three 1.1-pound containers; the two you are not using can be immediately frozen. I have found that the syrup extract will last for about eight weeks in the freezer once opened. But that shouldn't be an issue—we've provided you with many different recipes so you can continue experimenting. Once you've produced three or four varieties, invite some friends over for a beer tasting.

Beer yeast is readily available in 5-, 7-, and 14-gram sachets. The Nottingham yeast you received in this kit is by far your best choice and is widely available. Munton & Fison, Coopers, and Windsor ale yeasts are the other easy-to-find beer yeasts you can use. They are all fairly similar, although the Windsor yeast does not ferment as completely and consequently leaves a richer, maltier beer. Resist the temptation to use a bread yeast. Your beer will not ferment well or completely, it will always be very cloudy, and it will have a distinct bread yeast flavor. Yuck. Wine yeasts have been tried as well, however they leave your beer with a thin, winelike flavor often described as "cidery."

As for the quantity of yeast, you will only use 1 teaspoon at a time. This is approximately one-half of a 5-gram package. The remaining yeast should also be kept in the freezer, and will stay fresh for six weeks once opened.

We've talked about other styles of beer. What we need now are some recipes so we can produce those other variations. All of the recipes that follow are tried and true, and a couple of them are award winners. They will give you a good idea of how you can substitute items and create your own distinctive microbrews.

Some of the recipes call for adding your own hops at certain intervals. This is necessary because with these particular recipes you will not be using a hopped extract. Rather, you will be asked to use an unhopped dry extract or syrup, creating your own hopped wort. Each recipe specifies when to add the hops.

Hops are available in whole leaf or in chopped-up, compressed pellet form. There are advantages to each kind. Leaf hops are usually preferred for their unprocessed character. On the other hand, hops that have been pelletized are more readily available, easier to use, and better for extracting bitterness, especially in smaller batches with shorter boils. As you have probably guessed, I recommend using pelletized hops with these recipes. Straining out the hops sediment that will be created can be done, but is not necessary.

Manipulating hops in a beer recipe is not the only way to affect flavor. All of the malts—as opposed to the malt extracts—that are called for in the following recipes are available in the form of a grain. They should be crushed at the place of purchase, but if you forget to have them crushed, a hard surface and a rolling pin will work. Just beware that it can be messy. Do not use a coffee grinder—it will turn your grain into powder. Once the malts are crushed, they need to be steeped in your brewing water for 10 minutes before you commence the boil.

Alcohol content of your beer is directly correlated to

the amount of sugar available to the yeast for fermentation. If a slightly higher alcohol content is desired, add up to ½ cup of corn sugar near the end of the boil. Unfortunately, lower alcohol beers cannot be made without sacrificing body and flavor. Except where noted in the recipes, procedures and times for the addition of ingredients are identical to the amber ale you made with this kit.

The shelf life of a beer is usually two to three months, although beers with elevated alcohol percentages, like the Imperial Stout recipe that's provided, will be good for years. This is not to say that any beer's taste will remain constant. Quite the contrary—they will all change. Most beers start to lose their fresh flavor after two months, although this does not render them undrinkable. High-alcohol beers mellow and smooth out with age, much like a fine Scotch.

The following recipes will make one gallon of beer. To increase the volume to the home-brewing standard of five gallons, simply increase all ingredients (except the yeast) fivefold. For the five-gallon quantity, ten grams, or two teaspoons, will be the maximum amount of yeast required.

All of the ingredients listed in these recipes are pretty common and can be found at nearly all brewing supply stores. Any home brewer trying a new recipe should approach it like a cook would. We all have our own taste in beer, and the beers we produce should reflect what we want in a beer. Experience will always be the best teacher when deciding how to adjust a recipe, but don't substitute ingredients fast and loose when brewing. Nothing in beer-making occurs in a vacuum—there are always unintended flavor side-effects. These side-effects aren't necessarily bad, but it is good to be aware that a change here will effect the flavor over there. Keep detailed records of what you do and only introduce one variable at a time, so if you have an unintended flavor change (for the better or worse) you will know what caused it.

Happy brewing!

Recipes

Pooh Brew Honey Ale

1 lb unhopped light malt extract syrup

$\frac{1}{2}$ lb clover honey

$\frac{1}{2}$ oz Hallertauer hops, added at beginning of boil

3–5 dried juniper berries, added at end of boil

1 tsp ale yeast

$\frac{1}{4}$ cup sugar (for priming)

Let's walk through the actual production of the Pooh Brew Honey Ale. The steps described here can be used for all of the following recipes. Pre-boil 1$\frac{1}{4}$ gallons of water just as you did for the amber ale. Add the malt extract syrup and bring to a light boil. After the initial foaming, which should last 2 to 3 minutes, add the Hallertauer hops. Sprinkle them in slowly. You could get a burst of overfoaming if you add them too fast. This is especially true with pelletized hops. Lightly boil the mixture for a total of 30 minutes. When there are 3 to 5 minutes remaining in the boil, add the $\frac{1}{2}$ lb of clover honey. Be sure the honey completely dissolves into the wort. At this time, also crush the juniper berries. Add the berries with 1 minute remaining in the boil. After the boil, the wort follows the procedures for the amber ale with one exception: Once the wort is cool, you may wish to strain out the hops and berry sediment. This is not necessary, but will lead to less sediment in your bottles. You can strain your wort through a tight-mesh spaghetti strainer or cheese cloth, just make certain that whatever you run it through is sanitized. Also be certain your wort is cooled before straining. Fermentation is the same as with the amber ale, as is the bottling and bottle conditioning.

Uncle P's India Pale Ale (IPA)

A very popular beer style in the Pacific Northwest. Seattle and environs is hop country and this beer fairly screams with hops. Bold and bitter.

> 1½ lbs light dry malt extract
> ½ cup crystal malt
> ½ cup Victory malt
> ½ oz Centennial hops, added at beginning of boil
> ½ oz Centennial hops, added at end of boil
> 1 tsp ale yeast
> ¼ cup sugar (for priming)

Use dry malt extract as you would use malt extract syrup, adding it to the pot after you pre-boil the 1¼ gallons of water.

Wheaton Ale

One of the most popular craft beer styles in North America. Many Germans believe that wheat beer consumption, in moderation, of course, is good for the skin. This lightly hopped recipe is inspired by a popular Pacific Northwest wheat beer.

1½ lbs uphopped wheat malt extract syrup

½ cup crystal malt, steeped 10 min before boil

½ oz Tettnanger hops, added at beginning of boil

1 tsp ale yeast

¼ cup sugar (for priming)

I Feel Better Than James Brown Ale

A classic British-style ale. Sometimes made as a session beer, which means that you can drink a lot of it in one session and not fall off your barstool. Also lightly hopped.

1 lb unhopped amber malt extract syrup

¼ cup crystal malt

½ cup chocolate malt

½ oz Fuggle hops, added at beginning of boil

1 tsp ale yeast

¼ cup sugar (for priming)

RACHEL'S RED

Similar to the brown ale in bitterness and body, Cascade hops give this beer a distinct Northwest flavor.

1 lb light malt extract syrup

¼ cup chocolate malt

¼ cup crystal malt

½ oz Cascade hops, added at the beginning of boil

1 tsp ale yeast

¼ cup sugar (for priming)

THE COLONISTS STRIKE BACK PORTER

A variation of the well-known Redcoat's Revenge Porter, it was once described by a judge as "too dark, too rich." Could be.

1½ lbs unhopped dark malt extract syrup

½ lb dark dry malt extract

¾ cup crystal malt

¼ cup chocolate malt

⅛ cup black malt

½ oz Cascade hops, added at beginning of boil

1 tsp ale yeast

¼ cup sugar (for priming)

Mary Margaret's House Ale

When you think stout, you think Guinness. Well, here it is.
Or at least *my* rendition of it.

  1 lb unhopped dark malt extract syrup

  ½ lb dark dry malt extract

  ½ cup crystal malt

  ¼ cup black malt

  ¼ cup roasted barley

  ½ oz East Kent Goldings hops, added at beginning
  of boil

  ½ oz East Kent Golding hops, added at end of boil

  1 tsp ale yeast

  ¼ cup sugar (for priming)

Nationalist's Fervor Russian Imperial Stout

This style was originally made by John Courage Brewery under appointment of the czarist court in Russia. A big, bold, strong beer. This recipe is based on a beer that won first place in a large regional homebrewing competition.

2 lbs dark dry malt extract

1 cup dark brown sugar

$\frac{1}{2}$ cup crystal malt

$\frac{1}{4}$ cup chocolate malt

$\frac{1}{2}$ cup roasted barley

1 oz East Kent Golding hops, added at beginning of boil

$\frac{1}{2}$ oz East Kent Goldings hops, added at end of boil

1 tsp ale yeast

$\frac{1}{4}$ cup sugar (for priming)

RESOURCES

BREWING SUPPLY STORES & ORGANIZATIONS

Ever since home brewing was legalized in 1979, millions of beer lovers have discovered this enjoyable pastime. I have found that in the quest to brew great beer, a good home-brewing specialty store is indispensable, offering both good advice and camaraderie. If a store near you is not listed, consult the yellow pages under "Beer, Brewing Supplies."

American Homebrewers Association, Boulder, Colorado, (303) 447-0816

Beer Unlimited, Conshohocken, and Malvern, Pennsylvania, (610) 397-0666

Chicago Homebrew Supplies, Chicago, Illinois, (800) 231-BEER

Evergreen Brewing Supply Company, Bellevue, Mill Creek, and Snoqualmie, Washington, (800) 789-BREW

F. H. Steinbart, Portland, Oregon, (503) 232-8793

Great Fermentations of Marin, San Rafael, California,
(800) 570-BEER

Little Shop of Hops, New York City, New York,
(800) 343-HOPS

Stein Fillers, Long Beach, California, (310) 425-0588

The Boston Brewers Supply Company, Jamaica Plain,
Massachusetts, (617) 983-1710

American Homebrewers Association

At the forefront of the home-brewing hobby is the American Homebrewers Association (AHA). Since the early 1980s, this organization has been an invaluable resource for amateur brewers. Through sponsored events like the National Homebrew Competition and the bimonthly magazine *Zymurgy*, the AHA has helped pace the growth of the hobby. In recent years several home-brewing magazines have begun publishing. *Brew Your Own—The How-to Magazine* is one of the more accessible in both availability and content. If you live in a metropolitan area, you can most likely find an amateur brewing organization near you. These clubs are usually composed of home brewers who gather once a month to talk home brewing and share ideas, experiences, and, most importantly, each other's beer. The AHA maintains a comprehensive list of clubs in North America.

BrewSpeak

Beer: A fermented beverage made primarily of cereals, hops, and yeast. Ales and lagers are subcategories of beer.

Bottle conditioning: Naturally carbonating beer by priming, as opposed to the standard commercial practice of artificially carbonating beer by injecting carbon dioxide into the finished product.

Brewer's yeast: A single-cell microorganism that consumes sugar and creates consumable alcohol and carbon dioxide. Two distinct types of yeast are suitable for brewing: Saccaromyces cerevisiae (ale yeast) and Saccharomyces uvarum (lager yeast). Ale yeasts tend to ferment best at a higher temperature, 62–75°F, than do lager yeasts, which ferment more cleanly and in the 40–45°F range.

Chill haze: A cloudiness that can be present in unfiltered beers when they are chilled to serving temperature. Chill haze can be combated by the use of substances that prevent cloudiness. Since it does not affect the flavor of the beer, most home brewers give it little thought.

Fermentation: The chemical breakdown of sugar by yeast into ethyl alcohol and carbon dioxide.

Gravity: The density of beer, pre- and postfermentation. As sugars are converted into alcohol, the wort becomes less dense. Determining the gravity of beer will provide an indication of the progress of fermentation, of the body, and of the potential alcohol percentage of the finished beer.

Home brew: Beer lovingly and carefully made at home. The best beer I ever drank was the last one I made.

Hops: The cone of a perennial climbing vine. Hops are used to flavor beer and provide a bitter balance to the malt sweetness.

Malt: Commonly used term for the barley used in beer production, which has been allowed to germinate and is then kilned.

Pitching: Brewspeak for "adding," as in "pitching" the yeast. Not to be confused with the act of throwing a baseball really, really fast.

Priming: Carbonating beer by adding fermentable sugar just prior to bottling.

Racking: The process of transferring beer from one vessel to another.

Wort: An unfermented mixture of water, malt sugar, and hops.

Recommended Books

Wheeler, Graham. *Homebrewing: The CAMRA Guide* (Saint Albans, England: CAMRA Books, 1993).

Miller, Dave. *Dave Miller's Homebrewing Guide* (Pownal, Vt. : Storey Publishing, 1995).

Pappazian, George N. *The New Complete Joy of Homebrewing* (New York: Avon Books, 1991).

Wheeler, Graham and Roger Protz. *Brew Your Own Real Ale at Home* (Saint Albans, England: CAMRA Books, 1993).

About the Author

Mark Henry, along with his wife, Kimberly, is the owner of Evergreen Brewing Supply Company, with locations in Bellevue, Mill Creek, and Snoqualmie, Washington. He is a BJCP (Beer Judging Certification Program) Recognized Beer Judge, a monthly columnist for *BeerTalk* magazine, and an unabashed fan of the Evergreen Brewers, a Redmond city-league softball team. His column for *BeerTalk* and regularly posted personal brewing recipes can be found on the World Wide Web (http://www.halcyon.com/homebrew/welcome).